The Edge of the River

Written by Bob Hartman
Illustrated by Michael McGuire

For Sue, who watches out for us all. B.H.

To Katie with love for her warm inspiration. M.M.

VICTOR BOOKS
A Division of Scripture Press Publications Inc.

What was it like, at the edge of the river?

It was wet.

Squishy toe wet.

Soggy bottom wet.

Hot-and-muggy-sweat wet.

The girl peered through the reeds.

They sprouted thick and tall from the riverbank mud.

The girl peered out onto the river,

at a bobbing bullrush boat,

and hoped that her baby brother, at least, was dry.

Have you ever been hot and sweaty?

Sticky and soggy all over?

That's what it was like,

at the edge of the river.

It was wet.

What was it like, at the edge of the river?

It was boring.

She was supposed to watch her brother.

She was supposed to make sure nothing happened to him.

She was supposed to just sit there and wait.

But for how long?

Till Pharaoh, the King of Egypt, decided to stop
     killing all the baby Hebrew boys?

Or until her little brother started to outgrow his bullrush boat?

Till his arms poked through the sides, and his legs
     poked through the end, and his head popped out the top?

The girl laughed when she thought of that.

     It was nice to laugh, for a change.

As it was, her legs were stiff, from sitting still.

Her eyes were sore and tired, from watching.

And she could feel herself nodding off—feel her eyes dropping shut,
     feel her chin dropping onto her chest.

Have you ever felt that way—bored and tired of waiting?
     Wondering if that morning at school, or that hot afternoon
     at your Great-Aunt's, or that wait in the line
     for the bumper cars would ever be over?

That's what it was like, at the edge of the river.

It was boring.

What was it like, at the edge of the river?

It was looking bad.

The girl's long wait was broken by the sound of voices.

The riverbank reeds were broken by tramping feet.

And the hot sweat of boredom broke into a cold sweaty fear.

The girl crouched down as low as she could,

so she could see without being seen.

What she saw were women.

What she saw were Egyptian women!

What she saw were Egyptian women walking alongside the river,
    right toward her baby brother in his bullrush boat!

"If they find him," she thought, "they'll kill him."

But what could she do?

She was too small to fight them.

She was too slow to reach him and pull him back to shore.

And there was no time to run for help.

All she could do was watch and wait.

Did you ever see something bad about to happen?

A dog, in the street, in the path of a car?

A friend, in the playground, in the way of a bully?

A mom and a dad, in the middle of a fight?

Did you ever feel helpless,

    because you just couldn't stop it from happening?

That's what it was like, at the edge of the river.

It was looking bad.

What was it like, at the edge of the river?
It was looking worse!
The baby started to cry.
The women started to point.
And then one of them waded out into the river,
    pulled the bullrush boat out of the water,
    and carried it back to shore.

The other women gathered around and blocked the girl's view.

Now she was more helpless than ever!

And then the girl remembered. She remembered the stories her mother had told her about God. The God who had led Abraham to a special land. The God who had protected Jacob from the anger of his brother. The God who had saved Joseph from Pharaoh's prison.

Maybe, just maybe, she thought, *God could save her baby brother too.*

"Please, God," she prayed. "Don't let them hurt him."

Finally, the women moved away,
and she could see her little brother again.
He wasn't dead.
He wasn't hurt.
He wasn't even crying!
In fact, one of the women was holding him,
and hugging him, and stroking his head.
What was it like, at the edge of the river?
It was looking better!

What was it like, at the edge of the river?

It was time to do something.

If those Egyptian women were not going to hurt her brother,
    then the girl wanted to know what they did intend to do with him.

So she crept toward them.

Her body crouched low.

Her head below the reeds.

Her ears wide open.

"I am the Pharaoh's daughter," she heard one of the women say, "and I can
    do what I please. What will please me is to adopt this Hebrew child
    as my own. What I need is some woman to feed him and care for him
    until he is old enough to come and live with me."

Like a partridge spooked by a hunting dog,
 like a puppet on a stage, like a Jack-in-the-box,
 or maybe a Jill-in-the-box, the girl popped up
 out of the reeds, and said, "I know a woman who
 would be just perfect for that job. She doesn't live far
 from here, and I am sure she would love and care for
 your baby as if he were her very own."
Did you ever have the chance to do something good and
 brave and hard, but you had to take a risk,
 and do it right away, almost before
 you could think about it?
Well, that's what it was like,
 at the edge of the river.
It was time to do something.

What was it like, at the edge of the river?

It was time to wonder.

"All right," said the Egyptian woman to the girl. "Go and fetch this woman. Tell her that Pharaoh's daughter commands her to come and care for . . ." and here, the woman paused. "For my son, little 'Pulled Out,' for I pulled him out of the water."

The girl nodded, then turned and ran quickly home.

Now it was time to wonder.

How wonderful! Her brother was safe.

More wonderful still, his own mother would be able to care for him!

But what a silly name! Little Pulled Out.

What was the Egyptian word for that? Moses.

And then, she thought, *maybe it wasn't so silly.* Maybe his name was wonderful too. For hadn't she prayed? And hadn't the God of her fathers heard her prayer and pulled little Moses out of danger? Like He'd pulled Abraham and Jacob and Joseph out of trouble, all those years ago? God had pulled them out to do something special with them. And so the girl wondered: had God pulled out Moses to do something special with him as well?

And what about you? Has God ever done anything that made you wonder, made you shake your head and say, "Wow!" He still does that, you know. He still pulls people out of trouble, and He still gives them special things to do.

Keep watching and waiting, just like Moses' sister. And maybe someday, He'll surprise you too.

Other books in this series are:

The Morning of the World (the story of Creation)
The Middle of the Night (the story of young Samuel called by God)
The Birthday of a King (the story of the birth of Jesus)

The story you have just read is based on Exodus 2:1-10.
We encourage you to read the Bible passage itself and
discover even more about God's wonderful Word.

Art direction: Paul Higdon/Grace K. Chan Mallette
Production: Myrna Hasse
Editing: Liz Morton Duckworth

ISBN: 1-56476-041-3

1 2 3 4 5 6 7 8 9 10 Printing/Year 97 96 95 94 93

VICTOR BOOKS
A division of SP Publications, Inc.
Wheaton, Illinois 60187